OPEN

Written by Dawn Holden, September 2023
HCPC registered Paramedic. BSC Hons in Paramedic Practice. RCUK Advanced Life Support instructor.

All clinical information contained within this text is taken from current guidance published by the Resuscitation Council UK (www.resus.org.uk)

PandaParamedic
www.pandaparamedic.com

DISCLAIMER
All content and information in this book is for informational and educational purposes only and does not constitute medical advice. Although we strive to provide accurate general information, the information presented here is not a substitute for any kind of professional medical advice. The information in this book was correct at the time of publication, but the author does not assume any liability for loss or damage caused by errors or omissions.

PANDA PARAMEDIC

Learn How To Help When Kabe Koala Has An Anaphylactic Reaction

This is Panda Paramedic and her ambulance. She helps bears get to the hospital really quickly when they are super sick. Call her in an emergency!

Who is she going to help today...?

The cubs of Bear Town are all at school.

Beatrice Black Bear.
Sonny Sun Bear.
Billy Brown Bear.
And the twins, Katie and Kabe Koala.

They are all playing together in the playground.

Mr Specs, the teacher, has some exciting news for the cubs...
"As a treat for working hard and super listening, everyone can have an ice cream!”

“YAY" all the cubs cheer.

Mr Specs hands out ice creams for everyone.

“Thank you”, all the cubs are sure to say.

“Umm. delicious”
says Beatrice.

“Umm, divine” says
Sonny.

“Umm, delightful”
says Billy.

“Umm, delectable”
says Katie.

“OH OW” says Kabe
in a very concerned
voice.

Kabe suddenly becomes very unwell, very quickly.

“My tongue feels funny. I am itchy” Kabe complains.

Then Kabe’s face starts to **swell**.

Kabe sits down on the floor, leaning forward. He is struggling to breathe.

Katie jumps into action.

“Kabe is very **allergic** to nuts, there must be nuts in the ice cream!” explains Katie.

She takes the ice cream from Kabe and throws it away.

Next Katie turns to
Beatrice and says,
"Go and tell Mr Specs
to dial **999**. We need
Panda Paramedic
and the ambulance.
Kabe is having an
**anaphylactic
reaction**."

Beatrice rushes off
to get help

Beatrice finds Mr Specs and gives him the message.

Mr Specs immediately goes to the phone and dials **999**.

“We need Panda Paramedic and the ambulance. Kabe Koala is having an **anaphylactic reaction**!” he tells the call handler.

“We are at Bear School,” he explains, when asked his location. “Hurry, please!”

The call handler assures him that Panda Paramedic is on her way.

"Kabe needs his **adrenaline pen**" states Katie.

She reaches into Kabe's bag and pulls out a small box. Inside the box is the **adrenaline pen**.

Katie opens the box , takes the lid off the pen, holds the pen in the middle, and presses it firmly into the top part of Kabe's leg.

She holds the pen in place until she hears a click.

CLICK. The **adrenaline** has been given.

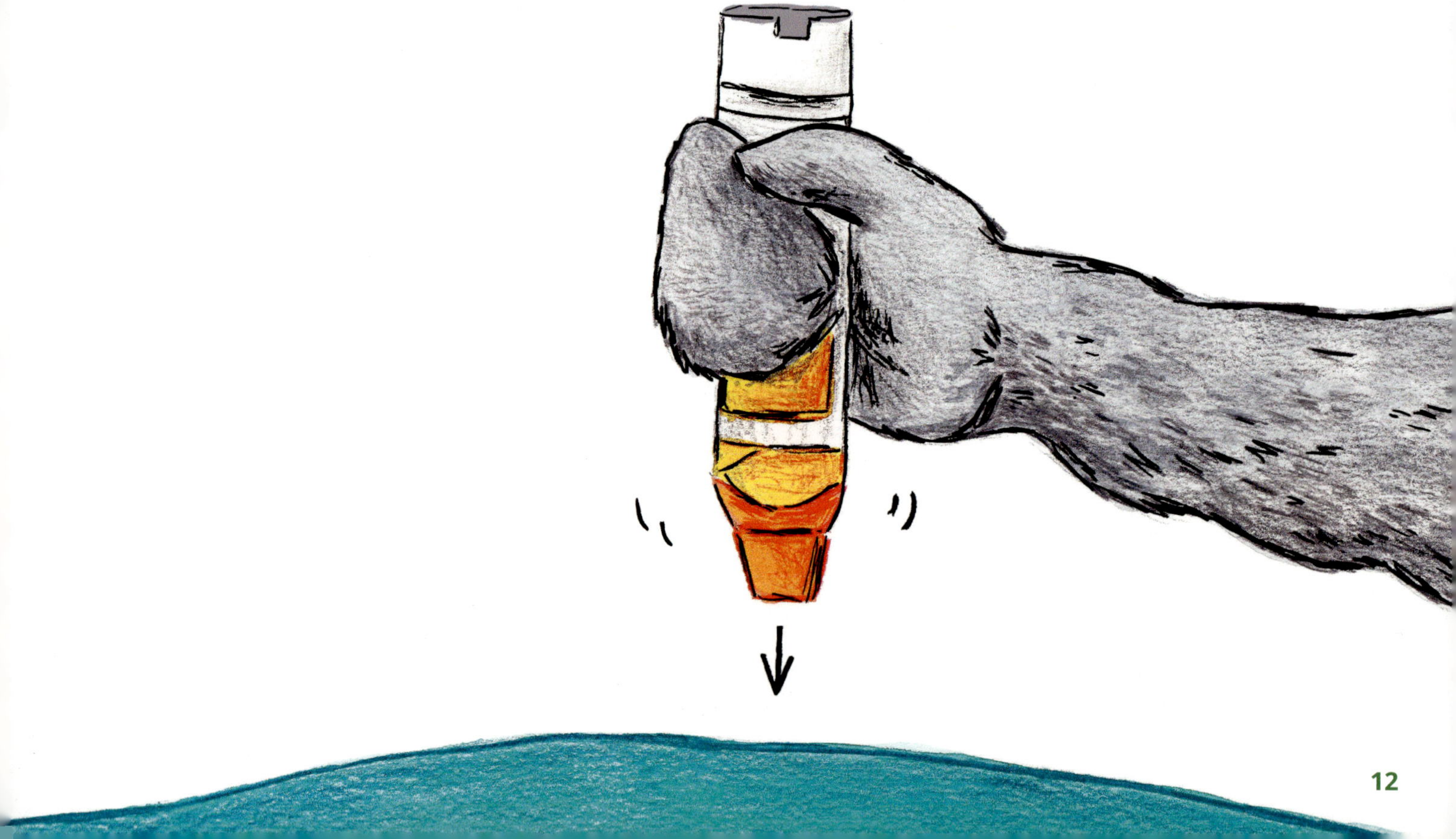

Kabe **collapses** to the floor.

He is still breathing really really fast.

Katie takes Kabe's legs and raises them up high, resting them on a chair.

"This will help his blood to **circulate** around his body," she states.

NEE NAR NEE NAR NEE NAR... here is Panda Paramedic with her ambulance.
“Hello, I'm Panda Paramedic and I'm here to help. What has happened?"

“Kabe is having an **anaphylactic reaction**. I have given one shot of **adrenaline**” Katie Koala replies
“Excellent job, Katie, and you other bears! Well done, using your lifesaving **first aid** skills,” says Panda Paramedic.

Panda Paramedic works very quickly.

She puts an oxygen mask on Kabe.

Then she gives Kabe another shot of adrenaline in his other leg.

Then she inserts a little needle in Kabe's arm and puts up a drip.

"Ugh ugh" Kabe groans. He is starting to wake up.

Mr Specs and Sonny hurry to the ambulance and bring the stretcher.
Kabe Koala is loaded carefully onto it.

The stretcher is loaded into the ambulance with Kabe Koala safely fastened in. Panda Paramedic drives to the hospital.

NEE NAR NEE NAR the sirens blare. She arrives at the hospital in super quick time.

"Hello, Nurse Moon Bear and Doctor Moon Bear. Kabe Koala has had a **life threatening anaphylactic reaction**. The **allergen** appears to have been nuts in the ice cream. He has had two shots of **adrenaline**, oxygen and a drip. He is not fully awake and is still really sick."

"Thank you for taking such good care of Kabe. We will run some tests, give him some medicine, and continue to look after him," says Doctor Moon Bear.

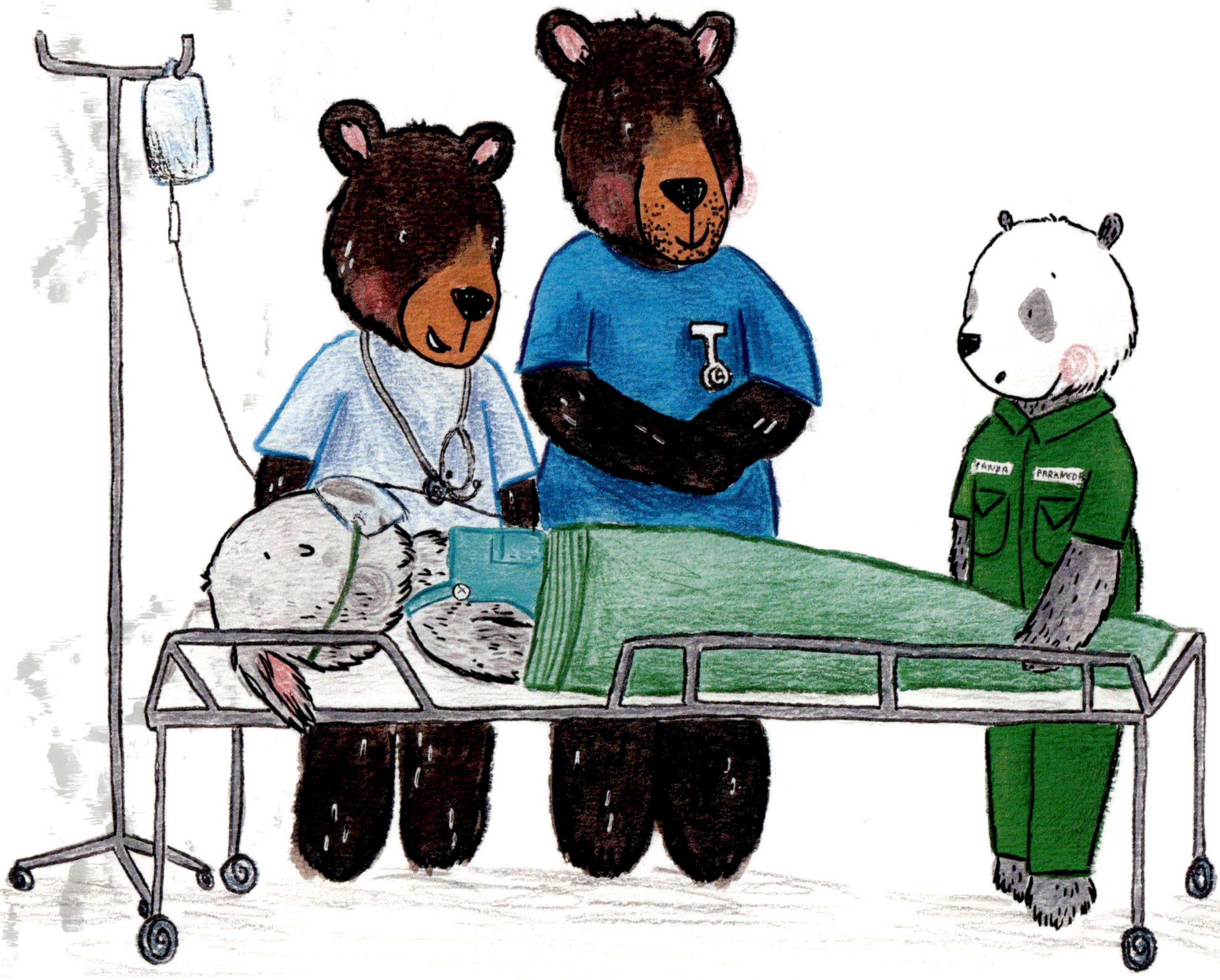

Kabe Koala is soon feeling well again thanks to Katie's quick actions, and all the help given to him by the bears in Bear Town.

Mr Specs and all the children have now learnt to always check the label on foods in case there are any **allergens**, as they do not want a repeat of yesterday's alarming events!

Glossary

swell - when too much fluid collects under the skin making the area bigger. During anaphylaxis a person can have swelling of the mouth, throat or tongue, which can make it difficult to breathe and swallow.

circulate - blood flowing around the body. Raising legs allows the blood to move more easily to the most important parts of the body: the heart, lungs and brain.

allergic - when your body reacts to an **allergen**. The symptoms can be mild (such as an itchy rash) but for some people it can be very serious (such as an anaphylactic reaction).

999 - emergency telephone number to ring the emergency services. You can contact the police, ambulance service, fire brigade or coastguard using this number.

anaphylactic reaction / Anaphylaxis - is a severe and **life threatening allergic** reaction that can happen quickly after contact with an **allergen**. The body's immune system (the system in your body that fights off illness) then overreacts to the **allergen**, releasing a flood of chemicals that can cause a person's airway to swell, difficulty breathing, and collapse.

adrenaline pen / adrenaline auto-injector - a device that allows you to inject a medicine called adrenaline. Adrenaline is the treatment for anaphylaxis as it will stop the reaction and reduce the swelling, which in turn allows the patient to breathe again. Adrenaline needs to be given immediately in an **anaphylactic reaction**.

collapse - has fallen down to the floor and will not wake up. There is no response when you shout and shake them gently.

first aid - is the help given immediately to a sick or injured person.

life threatening - when someone's life is in real and immediate danger.

allergen - substances that can trigger an allergic reaction in some people, such as certain foods (like peanuts or shellfish), insect stings, medications, or latex.

Fill In The Blanks

How to help a person when they have an anaphylactic reaction

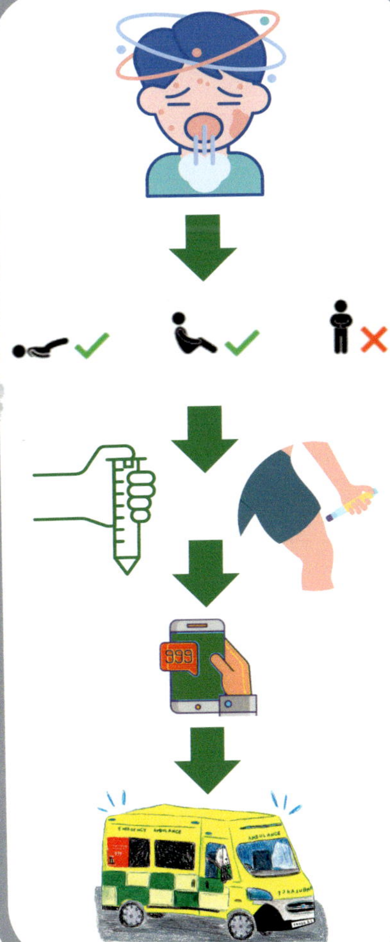

Recognise anaphylaxis
(Swelling to the f___ and tongue, difficulty breathing, feeling faint and unwell)

Sit the person up, or lay them down with l___ raised. DO NOT allow them to stand or walk.

Give an a__________ pen.

Phone ___ and tell them the person is suffering from anaphylaxis (ana-fil-axis).

The ambulance is on its way to take the person to ________.

Go to www.pandaparamedic.com to check out the answers

Can you spot 5 differences?

Can you find the words?

M	O	I	H	T	C	O	G	C	S	P	A	R	A	M	E	D	I	C	Z
J	H	X	Y	T	T	O	L	A	X	V	D	F	Q	V	V	Q	H	U	H
N	S	I	Y	Q	Z	S	L	E	N	C	T	C	J	A	Q	V	L	V	E
C	V	H	E	G	X	Y	I	L	K	A	B	V	U	S	A	I	H	L	S
Y	T	F	V	Q	E	J	T	M	A	U	P	P	S	Q	M	J	O	N	X
A	L	O	D	S	D	N	Z	V	A	P	Z	H	N	D	B	R	B	U	C
T	D	Y	G	E	U	W	Z	D	L	T	S	J	Y	B	U	E	Y	T	A
Q	Y	R	A	O	S	Y	I	R	L	A	C	E	Z	L	L	F	P	S	A
X	N	E	E	K	X	T	N	I	E	E	K	M	S	V	A	O	K	P	F
S	T	N	B	N	H	T	C	P	R	R	C	E	C	I	N	C	U	F	H
O	W	P	J	X	A	G	N	E	G	T	O	D	H	Z	C	H	T	C	Y
H	T	E	S	E	Q	L	T	F	I	W	Y	I	E	K	E	G	O	I	H
B	P	F	L	I	C	G	I	P	C	Z	J	C	M	G	A	B	Y	C	C
R	G	V	J	L	G	H	I	N	K	R	E	A	C	T	I	O	N	E	L
S	P	Y	A	L	L	E	R	G	E	N	J	T	R	Q	P	B	I	O	N
F	B	J	L	A	T	E	X	K	X	P	K	I	C	X	I	S	R	B	E
K	V	P	V	F	O	B	C	K	T	A	E	O	H	C	C	Y	F	T	B
T	O	A	H	E	Q	L	P	Z	D	A	H	N	V	O	V	P	E	D	I
V	A	I	B	I	G	Y	N	K	F	I	R	S	T	A	I	D	M	N	D
S	C	V	I	B	L	F	N	D	K	P	J	H	U	R	F	L	G	J	D

adrenaline pen	anaphylactic	medication
collapses	paramedic	ambulance
allergic	reaction	allergen
oxygen	swell	latex
first aid	nuts	drip

Can you colour me in?

CERTIFICATE
OF COMPLETION

THIS IS TO CERTIFY THAT

____

has succesfully learnt how to help a person when they have an anaphylactic reaction

PANDA PARAMEDIC

BOOK THREE

OPEN